# He

## Nature's Store

Julian Ashbourn

Copyright © 2017 Julian Ashbourn
All Rights Reserved
ISBN: 1978319592
ISBN -13: 978-1978319592

To Adrian and Viola

with Warmest Regards

Julia Alder

This book is dedicated to my dear wife Joanna, who, in addition to being an outstanding human being and at one with nature, is my constant inspiration in life and for whom all my written words exist.

# Contents

|   | Introduction | Pg 1 |
|---|---|---|
| 1 | Early Thoughts | Pg 3 |
| 2 | Religious Thoughts | Pg 17 |
| 3 | Scientific Thoughts | Pg 33 |
| 4 | Deeper Thoughts | Pg 45 |
| 5 | Final Thoughts | Pg 57 |

# Introduction

This book may at first seem shocking in its challenge to orthodox thinking, however, it is necessary to unravel and dissect this thinking in order to be able to see through the mist and strive to seek the truth beyond. There may be more meaning to life than just the continual churn of carbon exchange. The accumulated experience of life on Earth must surely have some higher purpose.

We should not be afraid to confront and explore these deeper questions, after all, they lie at the very heart of existence. If we cannot at least try to understand them, then what purpose have our lives served?

The concept of Heaven is a convenient model which emerges in several cultures. However, it is a model designed to fill the void of ignorance. Furthermore, it is a model which has often been misused to serve the interests of the politics of religion. Nevertheless, the miracle of nature leaves many questions unanswered, leaving an intellectual void which may, in fact, remain unfilled so long as the human species exists. However, that should not be a barrier to those who are prepared to think a little more deeply.

And so, in this work, a starting point is offered for those who have the inquisitiveness and openness of mind to exercise their powers of reason and think more deeply about such issues.

## 1. Beginnings

The question of what linked human beings to the great family of apes has occupied scientists for a great many years. Each hypothesis is sooner or later overturned by some new fossil evidence, often from the most unlikely of places, and often itself discredited upon closer examination. From time to time, nice, colourful charts are produced, showing a succession of ape like creatures gradually morphing into upright Homo sapiens who look just like us. Much is assumed in this context, often based upon fairly inconclusive historical evidence. The Neanderthals are perhaps the exception, based upon the quantity of fossil evidence, which also suggests beings of a higher intelligence than common apes (given the undoubted intelligence of modern apes such as Chimpanzees, Orangutans, Gorillas and others). But somewhere between the apes and the Neanderthals and Homo sapiens, there was another species which made the link. I will call these Hominids, as this is the accepted terminology of our times.

Defining a Hominid is not a straightforward task. Clearly, they must have been somewhat different from ourselves, and yet, also different from the other apes. Any description that we might offer must necessarily be conjecture as, the truth is, we simply do not know the nature of this link. I will describe a Hominid as being an ape like creature who had acquired the habit of walking on two legs, at least for most of the time, who was primarily a vegetarian, although not adverse to supplementing his diet with small creatures, and who had developed a certain capacity for organisation. Such a creature may also have developed a crude language in order to express both his feelings and his observations.

It is likely that, following natural evolutionary trends, Hominids developed in several locations simultaneously. This would explain the early differences between Chinese Asians, Eurasians, Africans, aboriginal Australians, Polynesians and other human ethnic groups, all of whom were subtly, but significantly different. In any event, Hominids must have been around for quite some time before the evolutionary branching to Homo sapiens occurred.

Let us imagine, for a moment, the world of the Hominid. He would have roamed across plains and through forests, would have climbed mountains and sheltered in valleys. He probably would have taken advantage of natural protection, such as caves or dense forest areas, where he could fashion some of the natural elements to better suit his purpose, as apes do today. He would have understood the eternal story of hunters and prey, without calling it carbon exchange. He would have understood the fundamental laws of balance and motion without thinking of gravity. He would also have understood the life which was teeming all around him, from plants and trees, to the hundreds of animals large and small, and the fishes swimming in the sea. He would have known which were dangerous and which were helpful by their presence. Indeed, his understanding of the natural world would have been better than that of many humans living today. Moreover, his love of the natural world in which he lived, would have been stronger than that of many people living today. He must have looked up many times to the sunset and the slowly emerging stars and found them most beautiful. He must have listened to the song of small birds and found it charming and entertaining. He must have quenched his thirst from the cool waters of a sparkling brook or mountain stream and realised the goodness which was sustaining life. Whether or not he had specific words for these things is of no importance. His love would have been one of familiarity and respect for the beautiful world around him. A natural world of which he was an integral part. And it would have been a love felt most keenly in the depths of his heart.

Certainly, he must have occupied himself daily with the necessities of his hunting and gathering way of life, but that does not mean that he was ignorant of the world flourishing around him. Neither does it mean that he lacked an aesthetic appreciation. An appreciation of all that was good and beautiful. Generation after generation, this understanding would have been passed down, father to son and mother to daughter, slowly being refined and developed over time.

We see this happening with animals and birds in the wild today. An inherited intelligence to blend with the knowledge of experience and to pass on, once again, to a subsequent generation.

Of course, Hominids would have also understood the concept of birth, experience and death, before rebirth among the same species, be it plant or animal. Female Hominids, at first, would have been intrigued, if not a little frightened at the state of pregnancy. And yet, they would have witnessed it often enough in the wild to understand that it is a natural occurrence which gives rise to a new life among the species concerned. They would have been equally familiar with death. Realising that a time comes when the spirit departs the body and the latter returns, in time to the earth. These things we may reasonably assume of a species that sits between the apes and ourselves amid the branches of the tree of life. But surely, if Hominids are the link, then they must have also developed intellectually from their own immediate ancestors along the evolutionary path, in order to pass on that characteristic to Homo sapiens, just as a runner passes on the baton to the next in line in order that he may take it yet further along the course.

The question is, what form would such an intellectual development have taken? As previously suggested, an elementary vocabulary of some sort, in order to point out everyday objects or the presence of other species may have been developed. A use of manufactured tools, however crude, would surely have been inevitable. A knowledge of seasonal navigation would have been developed among some groups, together with an understanding of when best to undertake such journeys. There may even have been barter between individual groups, perhaps for valued objects, such as precious stones, animal hides or tools. We simply do not know how advanced these Hominids were. If they were little different from apes, then the jump to Homo sapiens would seem too large. They must surely have occupied some intermediate position along the evolutionary scale of development. Assuming such a position, we must also assume a well-developed intelligence.

And so, the Hominid was an intelligent creature, capable of reasoning and appreciation and in tune with his environment. At least, that is how he shall be described for the purposes of this book. The various groups of hominids differed in appearance according to geography and how they themselves had evolved from their immediate ancestors, but shared the intermediate level of understanding previously referred to, and which gave rise, eventually to Homo sapiens.

Consequently, it is certain that Hominids would have pondered the question of life and death. They would undoubtedly have entertained a concept of the spiritual. That spark of life which differentiates the living from the dead. Of course, they understood that, at some point during pregnancy, the unborn child became alive and that, at birth, all being well, the child was fully alive and aware of what was going on around him. From somewhere, a life had been granted. A spirit had been given to the flesh and a new human being had entered the magnificent world. It was the same with other animals and this would not have gone un-noticed. Even the different modes of entry afforded birds and reptiles would have been well understood. The question, in each case, was from where did this spark of life, or spirit, originate? Where did it come from? Similarly, when a loved one or relative within the group died, where did that spirit go to? It would have been perfectly natural to mourn the deceased, as Chimpanzees and other apes do today, and believe that they had gone away. The body obviously remained, but the person, or spirit, had gone. Yes, but where? Where was it that all these people were going to?

The Hominids would have been unencumbered by the concept of religion which caused so much suffering to Homo sapiens further along the evolutionary path. They, no doubt, would simply have reasoned that the spirit came and inhabited the new born offspring and that, later, it went away again, probably to the same place from whence it came. Perhaps they saw this simply as a natural phenomenon. The same natural rules that govern all living things, from the plants on the mountain side to the fish in the sea, and all the animals with which they were acquainted. This 'other place' was no doubt nature's store house from where life was given out and to where it must return at the end of its tenure, whatever form it adopted in the meantime. One could imagine Hominids reasoning this out. Perhaps they also thought that this 'other place' was far, far away beyond the skies that blanketed their world, and which brought life giving rain and sunshine. They may even have had a word which they ascribed to this very special place which was the home of the spirit. Perhaps they considered this as one great spiritual pool, from which each individual was granted a small drop, before passing it back to the pool. Or perhaps they considered it as another land where all the spirits that had ever lived, lived again. Perhaps, maybe, they had an entirely different concept of the spiritual which does not occur to us today.

In any event, early Hominids would have undoubtedly thought about such matters and would have had one or more hypotheses as to the wonder of nature and the miracle of life. Their perspectives may have differed geographically, but probably not by much. By the time of the last Hominids and the first Homo sapiens (by which I include their very first forms) such an understanding would have been firmly established. In such a manner it would be passed, eventually, to the Mesolithic peoples who, quite clearly, had some well-established ideas in this context. By Neolithic times these thoughts and ideas had crystallised into some very definite views which, in some cultures, were so embedded as to define and steer the very existence of day to day life and the beliefs which formed an important part of it. Naturally, it differed by both geography and relative cultural development.

In ancient Egypt, even during the Old Kingdom period, these beliefs had become well established, with the concept of an afterlife, a place where the spirit of the deceased would go after their life on Earth was complete. It was a small step to consider that, the better a person lived their life on Earth, the more comfortable would be their existence in the afterlife. By the time of the Middle Kingdom, particularly under the reign of Senruset I and Senruset II, these ideas merged into a most beautiful tapestry of ancient Egyptian mythology, the belief in an afterlife, art, astronomy, education and the building of some magnificent public and monumental works, many of which are now lost to us. Of particular interest is the weighing of the heart ceremony, which was to take place shortly after death. This was facilitated by Anubis, the faithful jackal, who would weigh the heart of the deceased against a feather, which represented the good deeds undertaken in life. If the scales balanced, then the spirit of the deceased was admitted into the temple of Isis and Osiris for all time. If not, the spirit would be transported into the underworld. The ancient Egyptian's fascination with, and extraordinary knowledge of astronomy, would no doubt have played an important part here, particularly among the temples and practising priests. So much of this knowledge was lost in the great fires at Alexandria, that we can only speculate upon the detail. However, we do know that the ancient Greeks borrowed heavily from Egyptian knowledge and that the Romans borrowed heavily from both.

And so, from the Hominids to the early Mesolithic peoples, there is no doubt that the concept of a very special place, from where the spirit came before birth and to where it returned after death, would have been well established. It might have been thought of as Mother Nature's pool of life, from where a constant output was matched by a constant input. The wonder and magic of nature, after all, must have played a constant and endearing part of this period. Even the earliest Hominids could not have failed to be deeply moved by the beauty of what they saw around them. The moon, the stars, the sparkling streams, the myriad plants and trees, the fascinating creatures of all types. The sunsets and sun rises, the purple skies, the wonder of rain and the shooting up of new plants. The magnificence of tall trees, the wondrous forests, teeming with life. How could these things not have made an impression?

There are those who would question early man's ability to hold an aesthetic appreciation, just as they question the same in animals. This is nonsense, as anyone who has studied animals in the wild will know. It is hard to think of an animal who does not have an aesthetic appreciation, who is not affected by the joys of spring, or who does not demonstrate a liking for favourite locations. Consequently, the Hominid, if possessing a superior intellect, would certainly have had such an appreciation. It follows then, that the Hominid would also have asked himself what we would now consider to be philosophic questions, around the origins of life and the meaning of death. Hominids would certainly have mourned the death of loved ones and, perhaps, at such times, may have looked up to the skies or the stars and wondered if that is where the spirit of the deceased had gone. For to them, the skies were the giver of light and warmth as well as the life sustaining waters, so why should there not be a place beyond the skies where the spirits of all their ancestors had gone and from where the spark of life came down to enter into the unborn child, or other animal. It would have represented a logical conclusion and, in the absence of advanced scientific knowledge, would no doubt have seemed entirely reasonable. Would they have had a word, or sound, that represented this place? We have no knowledge of this, but I would like to think that they did.

## 2. Religious Thoughts

As Homo sapiens proliferated, they slowly began to cease the nomadic, hunter gatherer life style and settle down into small villages or gatherings of like-minded groups, who realised that they could cultivate the land for crops, engage in animal husbandry, and also engage in the barter of manufactured goods with visiting groups. Villages, run along cooperative lines, became small towns where centralised administration started to play an important part. As these towns prospered and became what we might now call cities, officialdom started to raise its ugly head and individuals would fight for control, understanding that they could turn the work of hundreds, or even thousands, to their personal benefit. In return, they would offer guidance and organisation. The power of superstition and folklore would have not gone un-noticed by these neo leaders and they would have quickly understood the inherent potential for control as, belief is a powerful motivator among the masses. Without this element of control, their leadership would depend upon a continual struggle among the strongest and most powerful families, with limited potential for what we would now call politics.

It would have been a small matter for those in control to cobble together a collection of popular myths, fears of the unknown, and new ideas aimed at keeping the masses under some sort of control. After all, this would have appeared a better option than disarray and anarchy. If these myths could be aligned with some sort of mystical individual, either living or dead and seemingly independent of the leaders, then so much the better. Consequently, the concept of prophets was quite commonplace as time slipped from the wonder of the ancient Egyptians to the disparate centres of the Greeks, Trojans, Chinese, Native Americans and others, before the early Romans appeared on the scene. In the middle East in particular there was a vying of position among several entities as powerful families and tribes sought to establish themselves and build their empires, to the exclusion of course of others. Landmarks, such as the early city of Jerusalem, became centres of such struggles, with power and control changing hands quite often.

From a cultural perspective, the Sumerians and others had developed early systems of writing, as had the Egyptians before them. With writing, the legends, myths and prophecies, could be recorded on tablets and held in temples, as they slowly blossomed into what we might now recognise as religions. Those who would later be called Jews, themselves had different versions of these religions, before Christianity came along, and, later, yet another prophet, this timed called Muhammad, introduced the Islamic faith.

It is curious that, even in those early days of religious doctrine, the hypocrisy and lack of logic of having multiple versions of the truth did not seem to occur to those who embraced the concept wholeheartedly. And embrace it they did. To the point that it set brother against brother and sister against sister as the most bloody and cruel battles ensued between followers of the different myths and folklores. Those who sought power over the masses could now simply align themselves with one faith or another, in order to reinforce their position. The coexistence of claims of royal bloodlines and politics, made for a powerful concoction that has lasted ever since, ensuring untold riches for both the church and political leaders as the centuries ticked by.

The common denominator of most religions was, and remains, the idea of an all-seeing God. The Creator of Heaven and Earth, and all the creatures that walk upon the Earth, with a special exceptional creature made in God's own image, which was of course man. Our own scientific intelligence and knowledge of evolution has since disproved this particular myth. Evolution is real. We can see it working all around us, even though there are questions which remain unanswered. To detract from such heretic thinking, the leaders of religions remodelled them into something which absolutely demanded blind faith, at the fear of being rejected and cast into hell, another mythical creation. The phrase 'the fear of God' stems from, and illustrates this concept of blind faith. But faith in what exactly? The written texts which have been passed down through the ages and which masquerade as the words of God? They are not the words of God. They are the words of man. Collections of stories, myths and folklore, collated together and written out by scribes under the instruction of powerful leaders. Naturally, they contain stories of magic and miracles, for this is the stuff with which to best influence uneducated minds. The abject dissuasion of any individual reason, often at the fear of death, simply reinforced allegiance to the religion in question. Thus was born religious persecution. A particularly cruel, unjust, inhumane persecution which, almost unbelievably, continues to this day.

Of course, the pill was sweetened and the control emphasised by the suggestion of Heaven and Hell. Do as we say and you may be accepted into Heaven. Don't do as we say and you will burn for eternity in Hell. Put this way, the concept of Heaven as incorporated into those early religions, would have seemed quite agreeable, especially to those who either could not, or would not, reason for themselves. And so, this place that they called Heaven (or equivalent term) assumed mystical qualities wherein one could be assured of living forever in a paradise, where one would meet not only one's immediate ancestors, but all the great men who had ever lived. Everyone would love everyone else and everyone would have all that they desired. This idea was at odds with the experience of humanity upon the planet Earth, where hatred, envy and betrayal were more common than love for one's fellow humans. In addition, greed would ensure that the greedy would never be satisfied and would always want more, never ceasing for a moment to gain it by depriving others. It seems then, that in order to enter this magical place called Heaven, the majority of men and women would need to undergo a fairly radical transformation and become creatures quite unlike themselves. Furthermore, if the balance and associated decision was just, then the place they called Hell must be vastly more populated. Different cultures had different versions of these concepts at different times, although there exists a remarkable similarity between them. Having been established, they, together with their associated doctrines and administering agents, provided the perfect foil for all manner of cowards, criminals and dictators to hide behind.

In fact, it is quite remarkable how many bloody wars, persecutions and mass murders have been preceded by solemn declarations of faith to one religion or another.

Of course, there have always existed a number of good souls who have attempted to wield religion and religious faith sincerely, and for the betterment of the common good. Sometimes, these individuals have walked among the masses and have genuinely done their best to help others, in the name of God. Sometimes, they have simply congregated into groups and become self-sufficient, such as in monasteries and convents, occasionally opening their doors to those in need, or going out among the masses to declare their faith and encourage others to join with them. However, these good souls would be good souls with or without religion. They could simply spread kindness and benevolence in their own names, without having to cite a God. Some undoubtedly do, and have always done so, no matter what time or place they existed within. Are these then, who have no God, barred from entering Heaven? After all, one of the conditions of almost every religion is that the individual must have absolute, unquestioned faith, without questioning the truth of the myths and stories that have been written down by other men. If they do not have, and swear to, this blind faith, then they are cast as an unbeliever, a consequence of which may have been anything from social exclusion, to execution or worse, depending upon the regime in power. Throughout human history, the masses have thus felt compelled to declare themselves a follower of one faith or another. Mostly this is because they have been born into a family of those who call themselves believers. More rarely because they have chosen to of their own free will. In any event, it seems that the primary purpose of their declaration is one of exclusion. To exclude others who are not of their particular faith. This exclusion may be practiced overtly, or covertly, often depriving others of what is rightly theirs by underhand contrivance. Quite often, along the path of humanity, this exclusion has erupted into unveiled persecution, betrayal and murder, sometimes upon a horrific scale. And all of this in the name of God?

It seems that the concepts of God and Heaven are inseparable (by whatever names they go by). The propaganda always cites the wrath of God and how he will bar the faithless from Heaven.

Alternatively, for those who swear allegiance to their particular God, he is supposed to look after them and protect them from evil. The phrase 'may God be with you' or equivalents, exists in many languages and in many cultures. Part of the bargain for blind faith is that your God will stand by you in times of trouble and deliver you from evil. If that is so, where is the God for all the animals who are treated so cruelly by mankind? Where is the God for all the children who are abused and misused in the interests of adults? Where is the God for the lonely and heartbroken? Where is the God for those struck down by terrible illness and condemned to a short and miserable existence? Where is the God for women who, in some cultures, are still routinely abused by men? Where is the God for the innocents who are betrayed? Where was the God for those who died in the trenches during the Great War? Where was the God for those who suffered and died in the Nazi death camps during the second world war? As they were robbed of all human dignity and herded into the gas chambers, did their God not hear their pleas? As the gas pellets were introduced and they started to cough and wretch, clawing over each other to try to reach the air which didn't exist, where was their God? Why did he not deliver them from evil as promised? And did their tortured souls go to Heaven as their twisted and emaciated bodies were shovelled into the ovens, one upon another, and burned. When humans create Hell on Earth, why are they not stopped by this supposedly all-powerful God? And for the victims, why are they not saved and delivered from evil by the God that they have been worshipping all their lives?

The answers to all these questions is that the various Gods and religions that they are supposed to represent, are figments of man's invention. Calculated to control and to hide behind. This is why they were written down using such ferocious terms and why, even today, they bleed hatred, injustice and violence that runs over the Earth like so many rivers of blood.

This does not mean that the individual cannot be religious in their own way and do good in their own name. They do not need the mythical presence of another to be kind, just and upstanding in every aspect of their life on Earth. For many such individuals, their 'God' is the natural world and the miracle of nature and of the life that they can see all around them. Their kindness and benevolence will necessarily cover all living things and will know no segregation or exclusion. By shunning the man-made religions, they shun the use of them to wage war, or to generate hatred and cruelty. The truly good man or woman needs no such devices to hide behind or use as a prop. If they choose to believe in a Creator, then that belief is their own concern and need not be portrayed to others. Indeed, it will be a matter so deeply ingrained in their hearts, that they will have no need to ever mention it, except within their own most solemn thoughts. This is a true religion. A code of conduct that the truly good will always follow, at any cost and regardless of any resulting persecution. Those who are strong enough to stand proud of mass propaganda, will be the ones who truly understand humanity. They will necessarily understand the natural world and the miracle of life. Consequently, they will understand that all things which draw breath have a right to life, and a right to be here on Earth. They also have a right to reason and not be controlled by malicious forces. With these rights go responsibilities. Responsibilities towards others. To cherish and protect liberty. To respect the domains of others, whether humans or animals. To help those who are less fortunate than themselves. To show by example, how to lead a meaningful, true and dignified life, without hurting others, to pursue truth and kindness in all that they do. And all this they can do without religion. Indeed, they cannot do it with religion as, if they adhere blindly to whichever man-made faith they choose, it will certainly prevent them from doing so.

And what of this place called Heaven? Is it only open to those who have sworn allegiance to their particular faith? If so which faith? And what about all of the animals that have ever lived. Have they no right to Heaven? For they are just the same as us (some would argue that they are more noble, faithful and true). Is this Heaven also closed to good men and women who did not choose to bind themselves to a man-made religious doctrine? And what of those who were evil and cruel and yet professed allegiance to one of these religions? Will they be allowed into Heaven's everlasting green pastures? It seems that the concept of Heaven from a religious perspective, is used mainly as a threat; 'You will never get to Heaven unless you behave as we tell you to'. The problem is that behaving as one is told often leads to the abandonment of all humanity, as we have seen at various times throughout history and as we continue to witness today.

It is of course possible to remain religious and noble on one's own terms, without having to submit to the imposed doctrine of others. For those who are strong enough to do so, perhaps Heaven is internal. A condition of the soul or spirit that does not need to be transported anywhere. Those who are truly good will perhaps be aware of this, as they would a comforting flame in the darkness, and those to who they are good will perhaps catch a subconscious glimpse of the same. One thing is certain and that is that the suggestion of a Heaven and Hell should never be used as a threat or as a mechanism to bind one set of people to the will of others. Unfortunately, this is exactly as it has been used, in every religion since those myths and folklores were first gathered together by primitive peoples. The idea of an afterlife as perceived by the ancient Egyptians, may have been subtly different. There was clearly a good deal of symbolism involved and it may have been that the Egyptians did not think of their mythology and temple rites as a religion in the way that later peoples would do. Unfortunately, we simply do not have enough information to reach conclusions about this. However, it is doubtful that they ever used their faith for purposes of terrorism, neither does it look as though they tried to impose it, by force, upon others. It is that which followed which became so ruthless, so disruptive, so cruel, so bloody, so treacherous and so blind to its own limitations. It remains so today in many cases.

And so, the concept of Heaven must be analysed within this framework, which is both historical and contemporary. Those who wish to cling to it within this context, will surely do so. But how many of these *really* believe and how many are simply going with the flow? How many ever question that which they have been instructed to believe since childhood? How many measure this belief against the reality of the modern world? It is said that there are none so blind as those who will not see. As individuals, we shall only see if we have the courage to look, and look deeply, at what is really occurring on Earth. If we seek a Heaven, then surely this would not be a bad place to start building it. It won't appear by the accumulation of greed and wealth. Neither by lies, propaganda and politics. Indeed, it has not appeared by the prophesies and preaching of those who would bind others to their religious zeal. But perhaps a light might be gently shone upon it by the application of love, kindness and justice. By holding out a hand to those closest to us, whatever their station in life might be, that they might similarly hold out a hand to others. If we have faith in humanity, then this is surely the concept of Heaven that we should be striving for. Some will claim that it is much too late and that humanity has already gone too far in the wrong direction. Some will claim that it is an impossible dream. But how impossible is it in comparison to the Heaven promoted by the man-made religions which is never seen and yet which you are instructed, by fear of God, to believe in?

# 3. Scientific Thoughts

There are many other ways of considering life after death and what might or might not constitute some kind of Heaven. From a biological perspective, it is interesting to consider what is happening when the body finally starts to shut down. We may or may not be conscious at this point, but, in any event, we shall quickly drift into the unconscious and, finally, at some stage, the spirit and the body will part company. Some have particular views around how long this actually takes, often positing that the spirit remains for some little while after the body has shut down, finally separating and drifting off, maybe after minutes, maybe after one or more hours. In this context, it is interesting to consider the experiences of those who have been pronounced clinically dead, while on life support machines for example, but who subsequently remember the conversation of those around them, even, in some cases, claiming to have seen the room in which they were lying. This would suggest a degree of automated consciousness which may still function for a while after the body has died. It is a subject upon which we remain largely ignorant. Nevertheless, it is an extremely important subject with quite considerable ramifications.

I have used the word 'spirit' in order to give a name to anything biological which does not constitute identifiable matter. Precisely where this spirit resides is also not exactly clear. It has usually been assumed to be within the brain, although more recent experiences with those receiving donor organs suggests that this may be an over-simplification. Many patients have reported finding themselves mysteriously 'changed' after receiving donated organs. Could it be that this spirit actually resides in all of our major organs? After all, the association with the heart goes back into antiquity and has been believed by many cultures. It may be that the brain is more of a complex clearing house for the nervous system, more concerned with processing practical messages than being the primary home for the spirit. And what of the liver? Or lungs? The ancient Egyptians used Canopic jars to store the vital organs of the deceased, clearly placing a great importance upon them. Often these jars would be carefully hidden within the tomb, further indicating their importance.

If we look closer, right down to cellular level, we find that individual cells seem to have a self-governing purpose to them, being able to take autonomous action where and when required. This can be observed and measured, although our knowledge of why this is happening remains incomplete. Perhaps it should not surprise us as each cell has its nucleus and copy of the DNA strand, a mechanism whose operation continues to raise more questions. We can often see *what* is happening, but understanding *why*, and what triggers certain reactions is a complex Pandora's box of switching alleles, recessive and prominent elements and a myriad of mysterious replications and other actions for which we have no immediate answer. The wonder of DNA and cell replication is the mechanism of the miracle of nature. Having decided upon the exact positioning and switching of alleles, the instructions are sent down through 'messenger' mRNA to be coded for the precise combination of amino acids which, themselves, will constitute a particular protein. It is now thought that even proteins include a feedback mechanism which can inform DNA and, in effect, request an alternative protein. But what consciousness controls these complex operations? Who is making the necessary decisions? It surely cannot be completely random, even though there is an inherent randomness within the DNA mechanism. If it was completely random, then nature would be a complete mess. A hotchpotch of half formed ideas that do not gel together. However, as we are well aware, nature is not at all like this.

The spirit of intelligence which specifies and controls all of these actions must surely be present within every cell of our bodies. Consequently, it must reside within each of our primary organs. Whether we call this spirit, or consciousness, or the spark of life, or any other name of our choice, it is surely there. When our bodies eventually shut down and cell replication comes to an end, it just as surely leaves us. All of this we can grasp and appreciate from a purely biological perspective. The question is, from where did this spirit come before giving life to a new progeny, and to where does it return when the life of this new being is over?

Such questions are considered within the world's various religions, but no satisfactory answers come to light, at least not from a scientific perspective. It has been shown by various experiments, starting with the famous Miller-Urey experiments of 1952, that, under precisely the right conditions, amino acids, the building blocks of proteins, could be created artificially. Those early experiments gave weight to the hypothesis that life really did start on Earth and did not come here as a passenger on a meteor, or some other cosmic body.

Given exactly the right atmospheric conditions, an event whose probability must be considered very low indeed, it was clearly possible to create life. However, a collection of amino acids is a long way from a complex organism such as a human being. The late Lynn Margulis, whom I had the pleasure of meeting, undertook an enormous amount of work in order to show how single celled organisms could have transitioned into multi-cellular life. Her carefully developed theory of endosymbiosis is now widely accepted, although it took many years for others to appreciate it. This idea provided an evolutionary genesis for nucleic cells to become, eventually, what we would recognise as plants and animals. But even with these steps forward, we are still thinking from a chemical and biological perspective and cannot answer the big question.

It is only too easy to consider the spark of life as the electrical impulses which, undoubtedly, flow throughout the living body. Similarly, to align these impulses with the brain and nervous system. Certainly, this type of 'spark' can explain how instructions are passed to certain areas of the body, to be executed by the muscles. In a crude manner, the parallel of a motor car's ignition system might be used, whereupon, a spark is timed to fire at a particular point in time, in order to initiate combustion of a certain mixture which, in turn, activates the piston and turns the crankshaft. A computer similarly receives and processes instructions, via a predefined programme which, in turn, receives input from the user. One could give a hundred more examples of messages being originated, sent and acted upon, according to the design of a particular entity. In relation to the man-made examples, these were all carefully designed by a designer or design team. But who was the designer of the human nervous system, and where did the first spark come from? All of the correct conditions and physical mechanisms must exist before the first spark can come and activate the organism.

We are therefore left to consider two separate groups of activity and meaning. On the one hand, we have the biological development which builds the necessary mechanisms and construction of the organism prior to the entry of life and consciousness. On the other hand, we have that spark of life itself. The spirit which comes and inhabits the body. It brings consciousness, personality and, often enough, inherited behaviour patterns, more pronounced according to species. Just how much of this may be 'coded' into the mechanisms of DNA is highly questionable. Certainly, the phenotypic characteristics such as physical design and appearance, lend themselves to being encoded into the DNA strand, although this itself must be extremely complex when spread among so many cells. However, we remain within the physical and mechanical realm when considering such matters, except, that we have no idea how the first phenotypic information of every first example of an organism came into being. The evolution of the fittest examples is a logical matter if one considers selective reproduction and fitness for purpose. Even so, the manner in which these variations are brought into being would seem very complex. Surely, it cannot be simply a matter of randomness? If it was, the whole model of genetic alteration, sexual selection and modification would be chaotic. Nature however is not chaotic. It would seem, rather, to exhibit a controlled randomness, according to intelligent design principles.

This thinking gets us no nearer to the question of life force and consciousness, except the acceptance that there is something more than physical and chemical interaction and the coding of genetic sequences. Recent research into the subject of consciousness follows a repeated pattern of considering how the brain and nervous system function. It seems always to assume that consciousness is directly aligned with neurons and the processing of transmitted and received information. It often makes the comparison with computers in that a code or programme may be accessed in order to generate a specific reaction, perhaps to a nerve impulse. Protective mechanisms such as the feeling of pain are often put forward as an example. Certainly, one may imagine nerves around tissue that is being subjected to damage or mutilation, sending a multitude of responses back to the brain for processing. The brain may then respond with messages to remove the organ from the potential for damage. Scientists studying such phenomena often question whether such responses actually require consciousness or whether they are automatically managed by the complex nervous system and brain. Examples are given of blind individuals who effectively steer around obstacles in their path, even though they cannot consciously see them. The retina and nervous system in such cases would appear to be working independently of conscious thought and direction.

Many individuals will be able to cite examples whereupon they, with hindsight, found that they had just executed a complex operation without even thinking about it and, sometimes, without being able to remember anything about it, although they may well remember something else that they were thinking about at the time. A quite complex example of this may be found in relation to driving a motor car, where the driver, following a familiar route, will arrive at the end and suddenly realise that he cannot remember anything at all about the journey he has just made. This may apply to just a part of the journey, or the entire journey. In such an instance, the brain is certainly instructing the arms, hands and feet of the driver and, no doubt, steering him through some potentially hazardous situations, although he can remember nothing of it. Indeed, I have experienced this myself.

Clearly, the combination of brain and nervous system, coupled to our senses, is capable of extraordinary things, even in an autonomous manner. There may be many reasons for this, including perhaps a more complex system of memory banks than we understand. If we accept that this complex mechanism can function autonomously, providing it has access to experience, then it makes an even stronger case for the separation of consciousness, or spirit, from the body. It is almost as if we have four levels of abstraction. Firstly, the low level DNA and cellular activity. Secondly the tissue, including our skeletal, muscular and functioning organs. Thirdly, the brain and nervous system which exercises a certain amount of control over the physical entities. And fourthly, the spirit, which may be further subdivided into conscious thought, personality, comprehension and that intangible spark or life.

Just as with religious thinking, a certain point is reached where the traditional explanations and suppositions become increasingly tenuous, similarly, in the world of science, a point is reached where no satisfactory answers present themselves. That elusive entity that may be called 'spirit' or 'the spark of life' eludes any rational thought that may be commonly understood and agreed. It would appear then, that the enlightened individual, after studying the realities of science, might usefully extend their own thinking and enter into a deeper contemplation of such matters, drawing their own conclusions accordingly.

## 4. Deeper Thoughts

Having explored religious doctrine and the scientific thinking of our day, a position is reached from where the individual may enter into and explore a deeper, more meaningful world of thought. In order to enter this deeper comprehension, the individual must understand the limitations of science and religion and be prepared to cross boundaries into uncharted territories.

The first stop in this adventure might usefully be the universe itself. What do we really know about the universe? Actually, rather little. We have explored our immediate solar system and have arrived at the concept of galaxies in order to explain other clusters of stars. With the use of radio telescopes we have inferred the position of more distant bodies although, actually, we have no certain knowledge of any such matter. We have assumed that the universe is expanding because someone noticed the Doppler effect between two stars. Any physicist worth their salt will know that this means absolutely nothing except that the two points used for measurement are moving in relation to each other. It is absurd to claim that the universe is expanding. Expanding into what? Precisely what is it that it is displacing? Nothing? If it is nothing, then there is nothing to discuss and nothing to theorise about. Once again, we have reached the limits of our comprehension.

Nevertheless, the universe is a good place to start for, within the universe, we have life. Geological life which, in turn, can create the conditions for biological life. But geological life is itself very interesting. Exactly what is it that causes a new star to be born? Theoretical physicists and mathematicians will speak about infinite density and black holes. The truth is that they simply have no idea, except that there is a chemical reaction going on that reaches a particular point and then bursts into a much more significant life force, such as our Sun. Once a star has exploded into life and thrown off matter in the process, the laws of gravity dictate that these chunks of matter, which have been imbued with motion, continue their motion in an orbital manner around their parent sun. As they coalesce and mop up smaller chunks of matter, they become what we now call planets.

But who designed this mechanism? Does it all happen purely by chance? Even if it was all a matter of chance and probabilities, the elements of chance have to be in place to start with. The chemicals have to exist, somewhere. If the universe itself had a starting point, then the necessary chemicals had to exist in order for it to start. So where did they exist and what were they? We don't know, so we come up with nonsensical theories such as the 'big bang' idea which, the deeper you look into it, the more absurd it becomes. The fact is that we have reached a stumbling block along our road of comprehension and are reluctant to admit it.

I shall draw all of these intangibles together and simply use the familiar word 'nature' with which to describe them. After all, the miracle of nature is all embracing, from the universal level right down to the single bacteria existing on or within another organism, or the beautiful, triple symmetry of an acorn cluster. The manner in which rocks, having been pushed down into the subduction zones at ocean edges, will emerge as metamorphic rocks with their crystals beautifully arranged as they are pushed up, as granite plutons, or some other representation, creating the very ground upon which we walk. The miracle of nature is all around us. From the geological to the biological. From a single bee to the universe. From the source of a clear mountain stream, to a mighty ocean. There is nothing of which we can strive to understand that is not part of nature. Sometimes our understanding is clear, and sometimes it is weak. In any event, the essence of it is nature. It is nature which controls the geological solar system of which our Earth is a planet. It controls the other planets too, giving Saturn its beautiful rings and defining the axial tilt and orbits of all the planets around our Sun. It is nature that subjects this same solar system to influence from other heavenly bodies beyond its own sphere of operation. It is nature which creates atmospheres and paves the way for another miracle, biological and animate life. Does animate life exist elsewhere in the universe? Who knows. What we do know is that with

Mother Nature as the great creator, anything is possible. And everything concerning our existence, including our thoughts and our consciousness, is a creation of nature and is ultimately controlled by nature. The consciousness and personality with which we are, as individuals, imbued, can only have come from this same source. There is no other.

The question is, from where does nature pluck these resources prior to distribution, and, in any event, what is the purpose of this continual churn of, in biological terms, birth, life, death and rebirth? The same churn may be observed from a geological perspective as the tectonic plates perform their slow motion ballet upon the surface of the Earth. And, no doubt, the same exists with regard to our solar system, our galaxy and other galaxies within the universe. There is continual movement, albeit aligned with different concepts of time. We may delve even deeper and consider this factor of time. Surely, time is only relevant when measured between two entities. Day and night, the passing of the seasons, the life span of a moth and a human being. Whichever entities are chosen, time is relative between and among them. The same is no doubt true of space and distance.

However, no matter how we consider these relationships, they all occur against the backdrop of reality which is created by nature. The manipulation of these entities, including those inherent within animate life such as homo Sapiens, must be undertaken from a store of miracles, among which is the miracle of the spirit. The physical remains of a mammal such as ourselves, may be absorbed back into the elements in a number of ways. Consequently, we might posit that all minerals in the universe come from nature's store and are simply shuffled around via the processes of carbon exchange. This makes some sense as, indeed, we may observe such a process in action. Similarly, from a geological perspective, we may witness the processes of weathering, mid-ocean spreading and other activities which demonstrate the constant churn of creation, existence and destruction, before coming around to creation once again.

With physical and chemical elements, an entire process may be mapped out, albeit in rudimentary form, according to our current levels of understanding. But the spirit? That is a different matter entirely as we cannot observe either its entrance or exit, to and from living entities. Furthermore, it is difficult to suggest a point in time, with regard to the evolution of biological life, when this spirit suddenly came down and imbued living entities. There is no doubt however that this spirit exists, that it comes to the living entity at some point, and, equally, that it leaves the entity at, or around the point of death. It must come from somewhere and return to somewhere. If we accept that nature controls everything, then this spiritual store belongs to nature. Our individual spirits then, are a part of this greater store from which nature distributes all life. We are granted a small portion of it at birth, and we hand back this portion of spirit at the point of death.

But what is the purpose of this? Is it perhaps that our particular spirit, enriched by the experiences of life, is returned in a better or more advanced state than when it was granted to us? This would suggest that, from a spiritual perspective, the species simply gets better and better and more adept at dealing with the trials of life on Earth. Furthermore, that its latent knowledge and art is ingrained ever more deeply into the pool and, therefore, into every successive portion that is handed out. It might be argued that this would explain why, on very rare occasions, individuals are born who seem to be enormously gifted intellectually and artistically, even though their siblings and immediate predecessors were not. However, the probability of this remains quite low.

Conversely, those that misuse their gift of life by embracing greed, dishonesty and evil will also be handing back their distorted and ugly spirit. If this returns to the pool unchecked, then what does this mean for the average spiritual content of the pool? Will the spirit base become ever more tainted with the darkness of those who abuse it? This would mean that each generation would receive a poorer spiritual content than the last. If one were to hold up the human species as an example, there may be much weight to such an argument.

In the world of animals, a similar situation exists. Naturally, within and among species, there exists a certain amount of competition for survival. However, anyone who has really studied animal behaviour will understand that they are every bit as 'spiritual' as human beings. Probably more so in many cases, as their friendship, loyalty and kindness towards each other is true and inviolable. When man befriends and animal, he finds this to be abundantly true. Animals may exhibit anger, passion and other emotions, together with the necessity to prey upon others, but they very rarely exhibit malice. It would seem that their little piece of spirit comes from a clearer part of the pool.

The existence of such a pool, while pure conjecture on my part, would explain a great many things. In particular, the giving and returning of the spark of life. In this respect the pool may be thought of as heaven. It is the source of everything and the ultimate destination for all the spirits that have ever existed. It is managed by Mother Nature who produces and orchestrates a great many miracles, including the miracle of life. These miracles may be seen all around us, although the staggering beauty and delicacy of nature's creations remain beyond our comprehension. However, the cornucopia from which they spring, must surely be the closest thing to heaven that we are capable of imagining. This heaven is not populated by human beings, but by a magnificent store of spirit and design from which all things in the universe spring. The elements which came together to create stars, came from this heavenly store. The conceptions of time and space were hewn from its design palette. Upon planet Earth, the conditions were put in place to prepare for the miracle of life, although, geological life was already very well established. While the life upon planet Earth may be unique within our own little solar system, there is no reason to suppose that it is unique within the universe. We simply do not know. Especially as we measure, calculate and imagine everything only according to our own comprehension. We do not even understand the communal intelligence of insects and other life forms, sessile or mobile, upon our own planet.

The heavenly pool may perhaps be dipped into to various degrees according to the wishes of nature, as the structure of the universe follows its winding path of change. We cannot visualise how and why such decisions are made, as we cannot really visualise nature. That it is the source of everything, is undoubted. The wondrous designs of nature that we see all around us have emanated from the very heart of nature. How or why, we cannot exactly say. I shall hold to my model of the spiritual pool as one of the building blocks available to nature. I shall further posit that, if anything akin to a heaven exists anywhere, then this is where it exists. This is the seat of all knowledge and understanding. It is the well of spirituality from which all of our individual portions is drawn.

Surely then, we have a responsibility, a heavy responsibility, to ensure that our particular spirit is returned to the pool in a better state than when it was received. All of our experience, our understanding, our good works and our love will be bound to this spirit as it returns to the heavenly pool. The ancient Egyptian idea of the weighing of the heart ceremony, before entering the spirit world, is actually quite apt in this respect. Their heavenly court of Isis and Osiris has parallels with my heavenly pool of spirituality. In their world, Anubis officiated at the ceremony. In my world, there is no ceremony as such, but, certainly, the spirit will be returned, together with its good and bad deeds in situ. Whether the spirits are segregated upon receipt, who can say? Only Mother Nature.

# 5. Final Thoughts

The concepts portrayed in this book are difficult for many to discuss or even think about. That is not surprising given the amount of indoctrination that children of all cultures are subjected to. In science, that which may be observed, measured and accurately described holds sway over any deeper philosophical consideration. Consequently, there are some areas which remain outside of this scope and which are almost taboo to mention. Most individuals do not like their cosy beliefs to be questioned or even looked at too closely. But to adopt this attitude is to constrain and stifle the human imagination and block the way to enlightenment. We witnessed many examples of this in the middle ages when many were persecuted, tortured and killed simply because they had believed in a doctrine which was not even their own. Depending upon accidents of birth and geography, the innocent individual might well find themselves on the wrong side of this persecution divide. It is still happening today, in both an overt and covert manner. Often, those shouting the loudest about prejudice are those who are the most prejudiced of all. In an age of political correctness, we seem almost to be returning to those dark days when decent, honest people were afraid to speak out about the injustice around them, for fear of being immediately accused of some unfounded prejudice. Furthermore, they will often find that both their professional careers and social connections will be adversely affected if they dare to speak the truth or question anything.

We have become a world of quislings who submit to the propaganda spouted by governments, large organisations and the media, without daring to question anything that the bullying majority claims as fact. Well, I do dare. I dare to question the absurdity of countries who treat their own citizens poorly while giving preference to foreigners who have no understanding or sympathy for the countries whose cultures they are effectively destroying. I dare to question the pseudoscience which we are bombarded with which, in turn, serves to dumb down entire generations. I dare to question the hypocrisy of religious doctrines which demand everything from their subjects while acting dishonestly and, very often these days, violently. I also dare to question the hypocrisy of the wealthy ministers of such doctrines who, together with politicians, speak of an inclusive world, while they continue to divide and segregate. I dare to question the inhumanity of the obscenely rich who prey upon the masses for their own purposes and who give nothing. I dare to question the sham of civilisation that we are currently living under and which appears to have penetrated the whole world.

Consequently, I am not afraid to question some of the beliefs which underpin so much hypocrisy, while also striving to illustrate the gaps in both our scientific and cultural knowledge. It is only by acknowledging these gaps, together with our own ignorance, that we may chart an intelligent course into the future for mankind. If we hang on desperately to the myths, folklore, lies and deliberate deceptions, then the human race will be finished. We shall destroy ourselves through greed, deception and stupidity. Choose any government you wish and hold them against this backdrop. You will find a perfect fit. Choose any large multi-national corporation, and you will find the same. Delve into any of our religious doctrines and you will find the same reliance upon smoke and mirrors and propaganda. Where is the truth that all good people must seek? It is nowhere to be seen, at least not in public life as political correctness and pretence has swept across the globe like a malicious hurricane.

How may the individual break through this iron curtain of ignorance and begin to exercise their own capacity for reason? One way is to challenge the orthodoxies which have proved to be so damaging to civilisation and to embrace proper scientific understanding.

It is no accident or whim that this book is entitled Heaven. By challenging this most sacred of indoctrinated beliefs, the door is opened to reason. Allow me to get straight to the point. There is no God. No celestial being nicely enrobed in the image of man, dictating events upon Earth. Such a figure simply does not exist. There are no pearly gates through which one enters the mythical place called Heaven, complete with angels playing softly on harps. There is no promised land. There is no dichotomy between Heaven and Hell. We are constructed of chemicals, with our bodies subject to the laws of biology, just as with everything that grows or draws breath. Everything that is imbued with the miracle of life. We all have a DNA pattern that we adhere to, we are all subject to the birth, blossoming, decay and death cycles and, in all cases, our physical entities, one way or another, return to the fundamental elements of existence.

What happens with our spirits is another matter. If, as posited in this book, they return to some central pool of spirituality, then it is that pool which is the true Heaven. It is there that the individual molecules of spirit, as granted to individual beings, began and it is surely there that they return. If we have lived our lives according to a creed of truth, dignity and kindness, then our particular molecules of spirit will perhaps be returned, enhanced by the experience of life. If we have not lived such a life, then our existence has been wasted time. We would have simply been imbued with that spiritual spark of life for no good purpose.

In this context, it is interesting to compare species. Humans, in a rare combination of ignorance and arrogance, tend to believe that they are superior to other creatures. But other creatures display a remarkable degree of reasoning and intelligence. They also display altruistic traits such as sympathy, kindness and loyalty, often well in excess of what is typically found in humans. It follows then, that they also have a spirituality and that their spirits are perhaps sourced from the same pool; Mother Nature's store.

But we must remember that some creatures and plants with whom we share our planet, were here long before we were. Consequently, their cycle of spiritual activity may be more developed than ours. Their intelligence, in many cases, has certainly evolved along different paths than our own. The communal intelligence and coordination among ants, termites, bees, wasps and certain other insects is beyond anything that we can master. Their communal organisation is similarly beyond our own. The complex manner in which many plant species spread their seeds, often with symbiotic relationships with other creatures, demonstrates an impressive evolutionary path. The complex life in the depths of our oceans holds many secrets, although it is becoming clear that many aquatic animals have a remarkable intelligence. And yet, we have excluded all of these other creatures from our folklore, superstitious vision of Heaven. Are they not entitled to the same grace and everlasting life?

Once we break clear of mythology and enforced religious beliefs, these ambiguities evaporate. The model of nature's pool of spirituality, holds true for everyone. The everlasting life is not individual everlasting life, but nature's everlasting life of its own repeated cycles. These will last for as long as nature decrees that time should exist. If, one day, our star, the Sun, should fade and die, then it will be as a result of chemical reactions, and all chemical reactions are a part of nature. If, before that time, upon planet Earth, human civilisation comes to an end, then it will be due to various chemical reactions that allow the evolution of homo Sapiens to embark upon a path of destruction. Indeed, there is good reason to believe that we are living within the leading edge of the next mass extinction upon Earth. All such developments would be caused and orchestrated, one way or another, by nature. Nature shall decree any fundamental changes in carbon exchange, via evolution. Perhaps it will cause life on Earth to be driven almost to the brink, before flourishing once more, in an evolutionary ballet which may last for tens of thousands of years or more. With a little imagination, coupled to solid scientific observation and intelligent analysis, such evolutionary paths are not hard to understand. The more we explore and, with open minds, learn in this context, the more archaic and ridiculous our various religious doctrines become, including the concept of a religious heaven where all those who swore blind faith to some words written by man, will one day end up and spend eternity in paradise.

There is no such place. There is only nature's pool of spirituality and nature's toolset. But these tools and resulting creations are in themselves so marvellous, so beautiful, so incomprehensible, that they represent more than all the miracles described within the various scriptures. Perhaps, those who can understand this, and set their minds free to seek the truth, are creating their own internal

Heaven. Their own secret place, deep within their hearts, which cannot be reached or tainted by the lies of man. Their own special place where they can feel at one with the powers of creation, and rest easily in the knowledge that they are, in fact, an integral part of it.

Those who understand this and who have created such a place, may perhaps be in touch with it when they walk deep into a forest, or walk far across the plains and then look up to the big skies above. Perhaps the howling of a wolf in the black of night brings them to their own special understanding and sense of oneness with nature. Perhaps it is the magnificence of mountains, or the innocent beauty of newly fledged birds. Whatever it is, it will be connected directly to the power and miracle of nature. Welcome to Heaven. That is, a spiritual Heaven which is our connection with nature. It can reside within any heart, if we allow it to. To feel it, we must first understand that nature is the source of everything. It is the source of geological life, of biological life and of everything in the universe. Our spirituality must therefore also come from nature, together with anything else that we attach to this word, such as consciousness or innate personality. It comes from nature and is returned to nature's pool, where it resides among many tools of natural elements. We may think of that spiritual pool as a kind of Heaven or we may cultivate a special Heaven within our own hearts. From our own Heaven, we may draw upon reserves of courage, integrity, truthfulness, kindness, compassion and understanding. As we exercise these good characteristics, we strengthen our individual spirituality, ensuring that our particular portion, loaned from the larger Heaven, will be returned in an improved state. Consequently, the Heaven inherent within our own spirituality is an integral part of the broader Heavenly pool.

However, all of this may only be realised if we set our minds free of prejudice, superstition and intolerance, and cultivate our imagination, understanding, and quest for truth. There is a universal peace, a universal understanding and a universal belonging. We are a part of it, if we can only see through the mist of our greed, arrogance, deception and superstition. Nature's Heaven is there. We can reach out and touch it, if we have the will and imagination to do so.

Made in the USA
Columbia, SC
22 October 2017